# Napkin Folding

# Napkin Folding

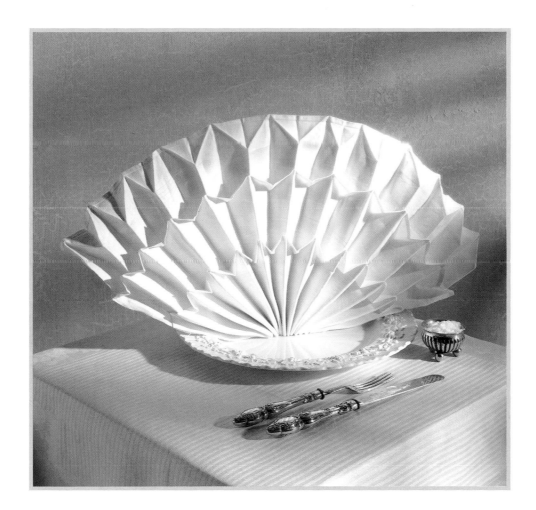

LINDA BARKER

a Salamander book

**Published by Salamander Books Limited**
**LONDON • NEW YORK**

Published by Salamander Books Ltd.,
129-137 York Way,
London N7 9LG,
United Kingdom.

© Salamander Books Ltd., 1993

ISBN 0 86101 690 4

Distributed by Hodder and Stoughton Services,
PO Box 6, Mill Road, Dunton Green,
Sevenoaks, Kent TN13 2XX.

All correspondence concerning the content of this volume
should be addressed to Salamander Books Ltd.

## ACKNOWLEDGEMENTS

The publishers would like to thank
The General Trading Company
144 Sloane Street, London SW1
for the napkins, china and
glassware featured in this book.

## CREDITS

**Author:** Linda Barker

**Napkin designs by:** Linda Barker

**Managing Editor:** Samantha Gray

**Copy Editor:** Alison Leach

**Designer:** Louise Bruce

**Photographers:** Graham Rae and Steve Tanner

**Typeset by:** BMD Graphics Ltd., Hemel Hempstead

**Colour Separation by:** Scantrans Pte Ltd., Singapore

**Printed in Singapore**

# CONTENTS

**Introduction**

6

**Decorative designs**

**Informal designs**

**Formal designs**

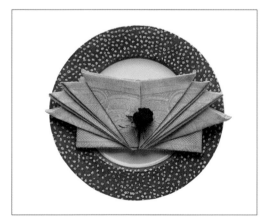

9　　　　　　　　　27　　　　　　　　　41

**Index**
64

# INTRODUCTION

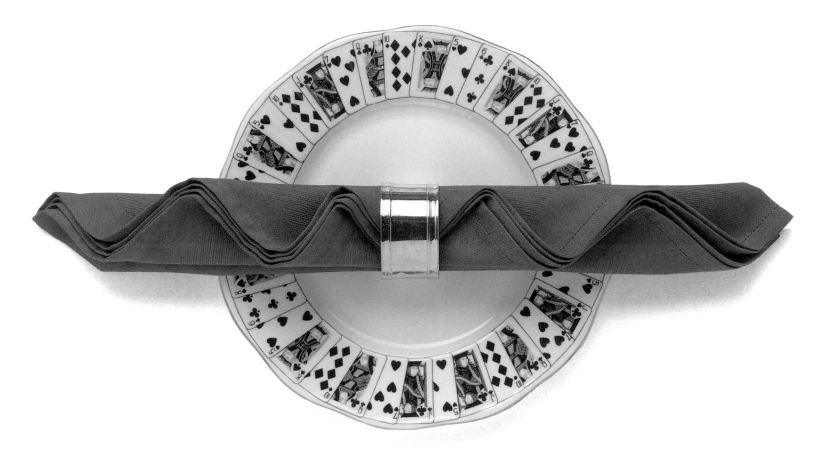

The Bow Tie's wavy effect is surprisingly easy to achieve and looks most effective when displayed on a decorative plate. Here, a silver napkin ring complements a sea-green, linen napkin.

The use of table linen can be traced back to the Middle Ages when it was fashionable to cover the table with a linen cloth and, by the end of the 16th century, the wealthy classes had begun to sit down to huge feasts at a more formal, 'laid' table. However, at this time, people still ate with their fingers and, naturally, the ends of the tablecloths (along with pieces of bread) were brought into use for wiping greasy fingers and mouths. It was not unusual for a tablecloth to be changed several times during the course of a meal and, when laid diagonally, the corners of the cloth were even tucked into collars! The natural progression was to tablecloths with removable linen borders, eliminating the need to change the whole cloth.

The 17th century saw the introduction of forks and the penchant for lavish meals. It was at this time that the first type of napkin was used – initially a vast piece of linen, long enough to cover the flamboyant clothing worn by both gentlemen and ladies of the time, tied at the neck.

Decorative, folded napkins were introduced in the extravagant Baroque era, and there were some quite extraordinary examples. Napkins were folded to resemble birds, flowers and fans and, on particularly splendid occasions, a different creation might be provided for each guest. These ornate table decorations, some of them permanently cut and sewn into place, were often kept from one meal to the next with only the more simply folded ones actually being used. At the turn of the 19th century many of the more intricate folds remained in use, although these were generally kept for the ladies, a simpler fold being used for the gentlemen.

Today, we are more likely to see folded linen napkins in restaurants than in the home. However, with the use of attractive napkin rings and bands, there is no reason why a stylish napkin should not be a part of every well set table for any meal of the day. The more elaborate designs are sure to create a memorable impression at a dinner party or special celebration.

# Basic Folding Tips

Creating a beautiful folded napkin is easy to do and there are only a few simple rules to follow and understand before successfully completing most of the folds in this book.

Firstly, ensure that hands and work surfaces are clean and always begin with an open napkin, placing it flat on the table in front of you. Try to fold on a cloth, as this will help the finished fold stand up.

When folding the napkin, always follow the instructions carefully, bearing the following points in mind. If the instructions tell you to fold 'down' into a rectangle or other shape, you should simply lift the edge of the napkin farthest away from you and fold it 'down' to meet the edge closest to you; do the opposite if you are instructed to fold 'up'. The 'top edge' is the edge of the napkin farthest away from you;

similarly, the 'top point' refers to the angle farthest away from you. Sizes of napkins vary a good deal, but it is recommended that you don't use napkins less than 42.5cm (17in) square. Napkins that are at least 50cm (20in) square usually produce the best results and a dinner napkin, usually 65cm (26in) square, is the ideal size to begin working with.

Cotton or linen napkins give the most elegant look and they fold best if freshly laundered, lightly starched and pressed. Napkins should be ironed flat and square at the corners. For the real perfectionist, napkins should be given a good soaking in cold-water starch and then mangled cold to obtain a stiff and dazzling quality. However, for the less committed, a can of spray starch gives very satisfactory

The Candle Fan looks dramatic unadorned,
or you could add artificial flowers to soften
the effect.

results, providing you do not use too much, or you may scorch the linen. Treated correctly, pure linen looks rich, takes folds well and is ideal for the more formal designs, while a cotton blend has a softer feel and lends itself well to more informal folds.

If you are fortunate enough to have lace napkins with decorative edges or embroidery, use folds that will show off their particular features. Many people like the look of delicate lace over a coloured base napkin; the two can be folded together for that extra special look.

If you prefer, all the designs in the book can be executed using paper napkins, usually available in cocktail and dinner sizes. Always buy the larger size and opt for the high-quality '3-ply' thickness. If you can only obtain the cheaper, thinner variety, fold two or even three napkins together. Paper napkins can be suitable for even the most lavish of dinner parties when given the 'all star' treatment with elegant folding and the addition of a fresh flower or pretty ribbon. Solid colour napkins are usually best to work with, as those with a design printed on only one side have to be carefully folded to ensure that the printed side faces outward on the finished design.

It is both fun and practical to have a variety of napkins of different patterns, colours and materials. Though you may not be fortunate enough to inherit lovely linen, your napkins will far outlast any piece of crystal or china. Generally, most spills and stains can be easily removed.

For that special event, it is worthwhile putting a bit of extra thought into the presentation of your napkin. Stencilled decoration can be applied with stylish results and thoughtfully planned designs can complement your crockery, your cutlery or even the food itself. A stencilled Chinese motif, for example, would help to make an oriental meal really memorable. For special events and celebration meals, the napkins are always more than protection for diners' clothing – they are there to enhance and enliven even the most minimal table setting.

**Above:** Shown off particularly well in a conical glass, the Double Cornet makes a handsome display.

**Left:** You can make this pretty napkin ring by simply threading colourful beads on to fine elastic.

# CHAPTER ONE

# DECORATIVE DESIGNS

For special celebrations it's worth taking a little extra time to make up stylish
and unusual napkin designs. Bits and pieces around the house can come in
useful for creating imaginative table settings that everyone will remember.

# Copy-cat Napkin Ring

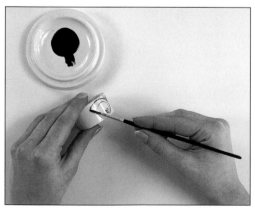

**1** Decorate some napkin rings to match your plates. You will need ceramic paints that match the colours of your china: in this case blue, green and pink. First, paint the outline of the design using a very fine brush and being careful to make a single sweeping movement with each stroke.

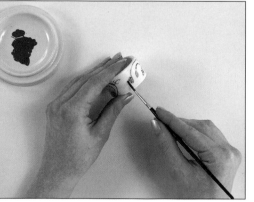

**2** When the initial coat is dry, begin to fill in the outline with a second colour, carefully following the design on your plate.

**3** Finish off with a third and, if necessary, a fourth colour, allowing each coat to dry before applying a new one. Protect the design with a coat of ceramic varnish. If you wish to decorate your table napkins as well, follow the same procedure using fabric paints.

# Lacy Napkin Folder

**1** Here's a quick and simple way to dress up a plain napkin for an afternoon tea party. All you need is a square paper doily, slightly larger than the napkin and preferably in a contrasting colour, and a floral motif. Begin by folding the napkin into a triangle.

**2** Fold the doily diagonally. To create a 'spine' to allow for the thickness of the napkin, unfold the doily and make another crease about 1cm (⅜in) below the first fold.

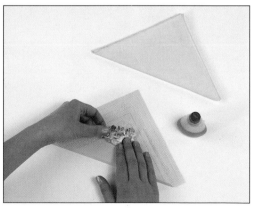

**3** Cut out a floral motif such as a Victorian scrap and glue it to the centre of the smaller (top) side of the doily. Insert the napkin.

# Thanksgiving Napkin

**1** This simple place setting is perfect for a Thanksgiving or Harvest Festival dinner. Use a sisal or straw placemat and a plain white napkin. For the decoration you will need a selection of dried flowers and grasses, and three lengths of beige ribbon, each about 50cm (20in) long.

**2** Tie the lengths of ribbon together at one end. Plait (braid) them until the plait is long enough to wrap around the napkin twice with a little left over to tie underneath.

**3** Group the bunch of dried flowers and grasses together, securing them with thread or twine. Fold the napkin in half twice to form a long, narrow rectangle. Lay the flowers on top of the napkin. Wind the plaited ribbon around the napkin and flowers twice and tie the ends under the napkin.

# Lacy Napkin Bow

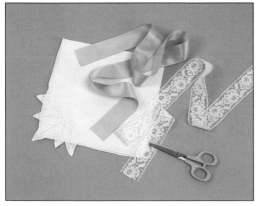

**1** Ideal for a wedding or anniversary dinner, this lacy napkin bow is not only pretty but also easy to make. The napkins themselves should preferably have a lace detail around the edge. For each napkin you will need about 90cm (36 in) of wide satin ribbon and the same amount of insertion lace.

**2** For the best results, the napkin should be starched and well ironed, and folded into quarters. To cut decorative points for the ribbon and lace, fold the ends as shown and cut them diagonally.

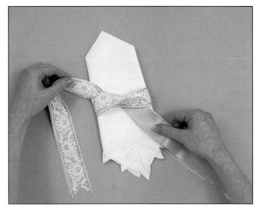

**3** Fold under two corners of the napkin to overlap in the centre, forming the shape shown here. Iron the folds flat. Lay the ribbon and lace flat, wrong side up, with the ribbon on top. Place the napkin on top and tie the ribbon and lace around it in a bow.

# Festive Napkin Rings

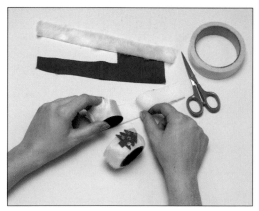

**1** Make some especially festive napkin rings for Christmas. Each one is made from a piece of cardboard tubing. Stick a strip of fake fur to the outside, to represent snow, and green felt to disguise the cardboard on the inside. Top it with a tiny green felt Christmas tree sparkling with sequins.

**2** The leaf sprig ring is first covered with a strip of sticky-backed plastic. Cut the plastic wide enough to go over to the inside of the ring, and cover the inside with a thinner strip of ribbon. The leaf design with a red bow is a Christmas cake decoration.

**3** Still another idea is to cover the ring with a small strip of wide satin ribbon. Glue a piece of narrower toning ribbon to the inside, folding the edges of the wide ribbon under as you go. Lastly, tie a strand of tinsel wire around the ring and finish with a bow.

# Tassel Napkin Ring

**1** This tasselled napkin ring is ideal for a special occasion. You will need two tassels and about 40cm (16in) of cord per napkin, and a strong fabric glue. Attach the tassels to the cord by wrapping the loop around the cord and pulling the tassel through it.

**2** Make the ring by feeding the cord through both loops of the tassels twice more. Make sure that the ring is large enough to slip easily over the napkin.

**3** Using a strong glue, secure the ends of the cord to the back of the ring. Lay one end along the back and trim it. Having applied the glue to the inside of the ring as shown, wrap the remaining end over the cords, covering the trimmed end. Cut the remaining cord on the inside, and clamp in place until dry.

# Floral Napkin Ring

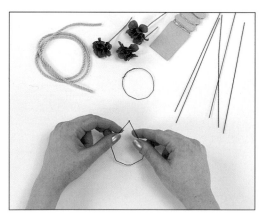

**1** This charming flower-trimmed napkin ring adds a touch of elegance to a table setting and is very easy to make. Bend a short length of florists' wire into a circle and twist the ends together to secure them.

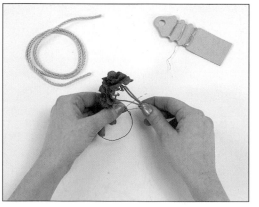

**2** Wind some fine fuse wire around one or two small silk flowers – chosen to co-ordinate with your china and table linen. Then twist the ends of the fuse wire around the circle of florists' wire to hold the flowers in place.

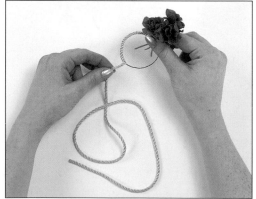

**3** Use narrow decorative braid to cover the wire. Hold one end in place with one hand, and use the other hand to twist the braid around the circle to cover it, beginning and ending underneath the flowers. Secure the ends with glue. Insert the napkin and add a fresh flower.

# Stencilled Shell Napkin

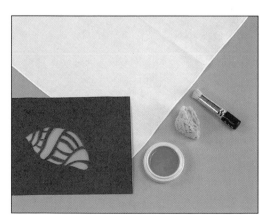

**1** You can easily decorate your own napkins with a stencil design to complement your china or decorative scheme. All you need is a plain napkin or a hemmed square of fabric, a stencil motif (either bought or original), a natural sponge and some fabric paint.

**2** Position the stencil on the napkin. Mix the paint in a saucer. Dip the sponge into the paint and dab it on a piece of scrap paper to remove the excess. Alternatively, you can use a stencil brush, which will give a slightly different effect from a sponge.

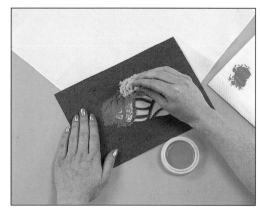

**3** You can either hold the stencil in place with your fingers or fasten it with sticky tape. Dab paint through the stencil onto the fabric, taking care that it doesn't seep under the edges. When the paint is dry, fix it following the manufacturer's instructions.

# Golden Leaves

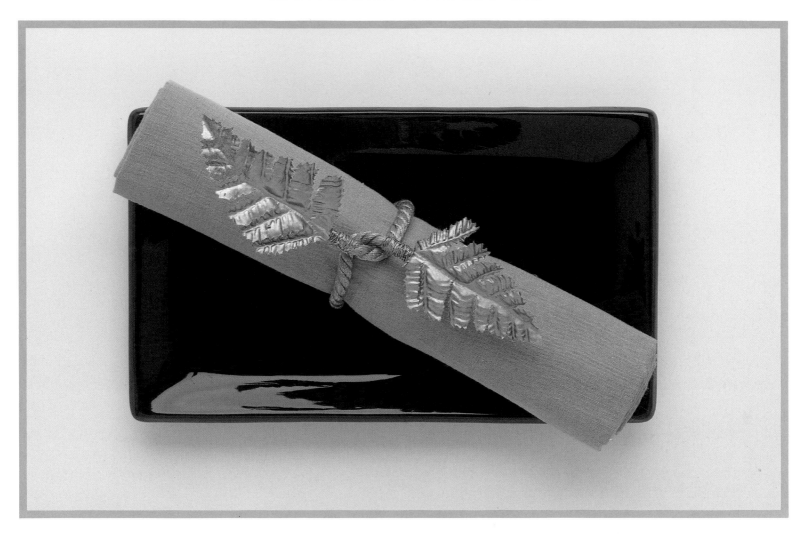

**1** This is a very stylish napkin idea and is ideal for a special dinner party. You will need enough florists' wire to wrap around each napkin one and a half times. Paint or spray silk fern leaves gold, allowing two leaves for each napkin. Leave to dry completely.

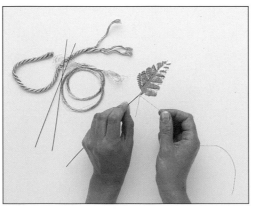

**2** Twist the ends of the wire around the stems of the fern leaves, securing them tightly, so that they can be curved easily.

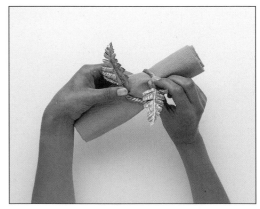

**3** Cover the wire completely using fine gold braid or ribbon. Twist tightly so the braid will not unravel and stick it down at regular intervals with glue. Twist the wire loosely around a rolled napkin with the leaves uppermost.

# Stiffened Bow

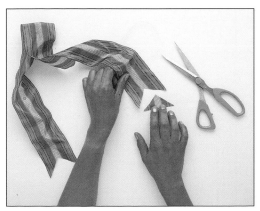

**1** This attractive napkin ring will add instant charm to any table setting. You will need 90cm (36 in) ribbon for each napkin. Choose a ribbon to match your china. Cut the ends of the ribbon into points by folding them double and cutting a diagonal across the fold.

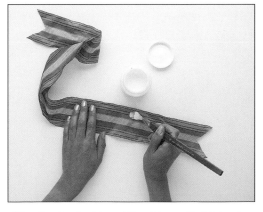

**2** Coat both sides of the ribbon with fabric glue and tie a bow loosely around a glass bottle that has a diameter similar to that of the napkin roll. Leave until almost dry.

**3** Slide the ring off the bottle and leave until completely dry. Insert a napkin that has been loosely rolled.

# Ribboned Napkin Ring

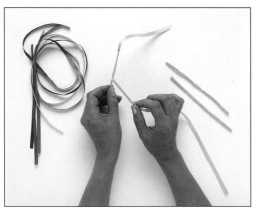

**1** This attractive napkin ring makes use of various lengths of ribbon that might otherwise be thrown away. Measure the circumference of a napkin ring and cut a pipe cleaner to this size. Wrap a length of ribbon tightly around the pipe cleaner, leaving a piece of ribbon free at each end. Secure the ribbon with thread.

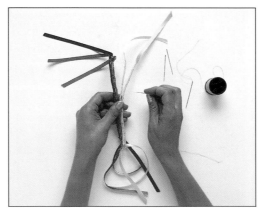

**2** Cover four or five matching lengths of pipe cleaner in the same way, using different colours of ribbon. Then sew each length together carefully to make a multi-coloured band.

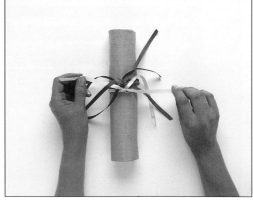

**3** Shape the band round to form a ring and insert a napkin. Tie each ribbon securely, allowing the ends to curl as shown.

# Jewelled Napkin Ring

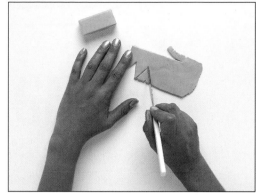

**1** This napkin ring will add sparkle to any table setting for a special occasion. You will need a small block of air-drying modelling clay, available at most art and craft stores. Roll out the clay and form it into a ring. A crown shape is shown in the photograph but you can sculpt any design you wish.

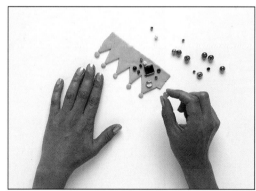

**2** While the clay is still soft, press a selection of multi-coloured gems or beads into the ring and leave to dry.

**3** Paint the bare parts of the ring decoratively, taking care not to touch the gems or beads, and leave to dry. Brush the ring with acrylic varnish to protect it.

# The Ruffle

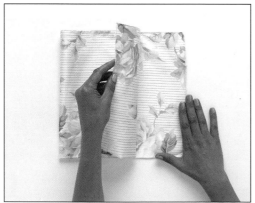

**1** Floral chintz napkins with this pretty fold are perfect for a summer tea party in the garden. Fold the napkin in half left to right and in half again top to bottom. Place in front of you with the open corners pointing upwards.

**2** Fold the first layer down and pleat it four times. Repeat with the second layer, placing this above the first layer of pleats. Press.

**3** Turn the napkin so the pleats are vertical. Fold the napkin in half with the pleats on the outside and arrange on a plate.

# Everyday Fold

**1** This looks pretty on the breakfast, lunch or dinner table, with toast or bread roll kept warm inside the pouch. Start by folding the napkin into three, then fold down the left- and right-hand edges as shown.

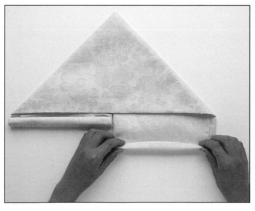

**2** Turn the napkin over and roll up the two overhanging edges tightly to the base of the triangle. Fold across the centre so that the rolled edges are on the outside.

**3** Hold the napkin by the rolled section and squash the farthest part of the triangle across the diagonal and open out the napkin. Place on a plate.

# Breakfast Fold

**1** Let the children paint a section of a cardboard tube for the napkin ring and display the prepared napkin on a breakfast tray. Fold the four corners into the centre and fold in half left to right and in half again bottom to top to make a small square.

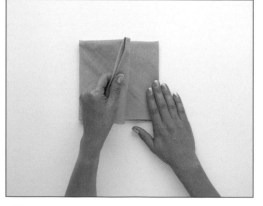

**2** Fold the top layer of the right-hand corner down and fold back the top left- and bottom right-hand corners, tucking them in neatly behind the napkin.

**3** Press the sides back and slip the napkin through the ring until the lower flap just covers the top of the ring.

# Envelope

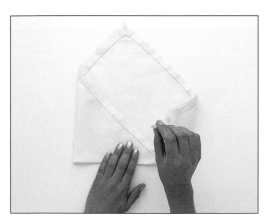

**1** Always popular with children, any number of treats can be hidden within the folds of this napkin. Adults might prefer a flower as shown in the main photograph! Fold the napkin in half across the diagonal, then fold the two outside edges into thirds along the lower edge.

**2** Place a finger over the centre of the napkin across all thicknesses and fold back the right-hand flap across the centre, squashing down the triangular flap to make a small diamond shape as shown.

**3** Fold down the top point of the napkin and tuck it into the diamond shape to close the envelope. Insert a flower if wished.

# Circular Napkin

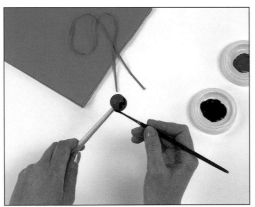

**1** This original napkin fold has a bead and ribbon trimming. Paint a plain 25mm (1in) wooden bead with a water-based paint to match your napkin. Allow to dry. Then paint on a pattern in a harmonizing or contrasting colour.

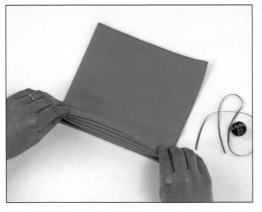

**2** Fold the napkin in half once along its length, and then pleat it accordion-style along its length, making sure that the folds are all exactly the same size.

**3** Thread a length of narrow ribbon through the bead and tie it to hold the bead in place. Wrap the ribbon around the centre of the napkin and tie it in a neat bow just below the bead. Fan the napkin out so that it forms a full circle.

# The Sailing Boat

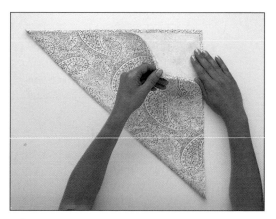

**1** A smaller napkin may be used for this fold and it works equally well with linen or paper. Start by folding the napkin in half diagonally.

**2** With the base of the triangle nearest you, roll the base up towards the top of the triangle. Roll as tightly as you can and stop rolling approximately 6.5cm (2½in) from the top point.

**3** Fold the napkin in half with the rolled edge inwards and arrange the boat on a plate with the edge extending over the rim.

# Deco Fold

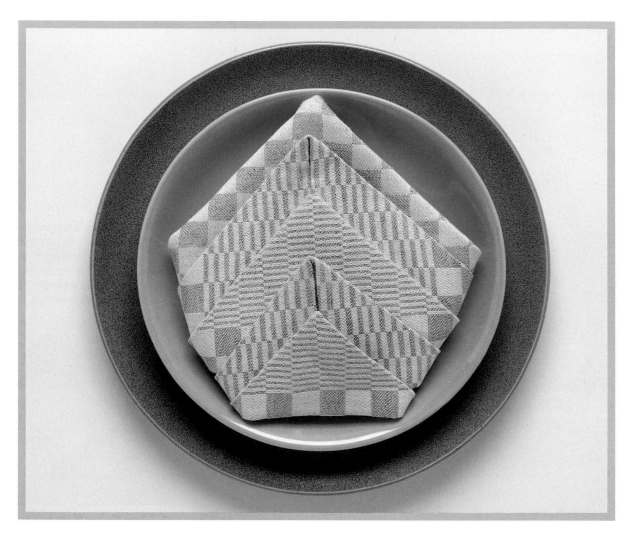

**1** Spray a large dinner napkin with a little starch to hold the folds for this design. Fold the four corners to meet in the centre, then fold in half left to right and in half again top to bottom to make a small square. Place the square in front of you so the points are facing down.

**2** Bring the single top layer up to the top point leaving a gap of 1.25cm (½in) at the top. Repeat with the three remaining layers, leaving an equal space between each layer.

**3** Fold back the left and right sides to create the final shape as shown and arrange on a plate with the base nearest you.

# The Umbrella

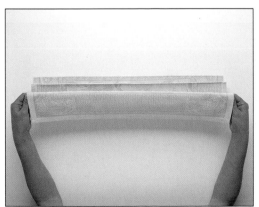

**1** A crisply starched napkin is required for this very attractive fold. Pleat the napkin into six equal 'concertina' folds.

**2** Tuck each fold in on itself at right angles and carefully press flat each triangular pocket that has been formed.

**3** Hold the bottom left- and right-hand corners and fold the napkin across so that the two held points meet in the centre of the napkin. Open up the folds and arrange the pleats outwards. Place the napkin on a plate and lay a flower in the centre, if liked.

# The Fan

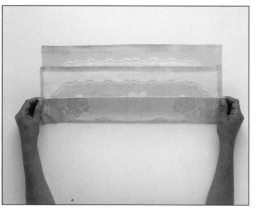

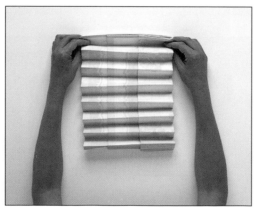

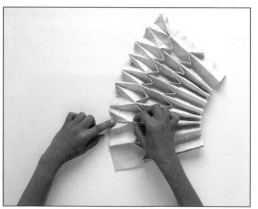

**1** This is definitely the napkin to impress! Start with a large, well starched napkin and fold the lower edge up towards the top edge, leaving a space of 5cm (2in). Fold up the new lower edge, again leaving a space of 5cm (2in).

**2** Pleat the napkin from left to right, concertina-style, pressing the folds firmly each time.

**3** Hold the napkin at the base and pull forward the edges on the bottom row where the pleats have been folded backwards, to make tiny triangular pockets. Continue along all the pleats on the bottom row and repeat the same process on the middle row, pressing the pockets. On the top row, fold the forward-facing pleats to make similar triangular pockets, facing backwards. Close the fan and press. Open the fan and arrange as shown.

# The Butterfly

**1** A crisply starched napkin is required for this pretty fold. Lay the napkin flat. Fold two edges to meet in the centre as shown. Then fold the half nearest you across the centre line and over on the top of the other half, to form a long, narrow rectangle.

**2** Fold the right-hand end of the rectangle in towards the centre, and with another fold double it back on itself as shown. Repeat with the left-hand side so that the double folds meet in the centre.

**3** Pull the right-hand back corner across to the left, bringing the front edge across the centre line to form a triangle. Holding the right-hand side with one hand, use the other hand to fold the corner back to its original position, thus creating the 'wings' of the butterfly. Repeat the procedure on the left-hand side so that the napkin has two symmetrical wings you can arrange to look like the completed fold, shown above.

# Index

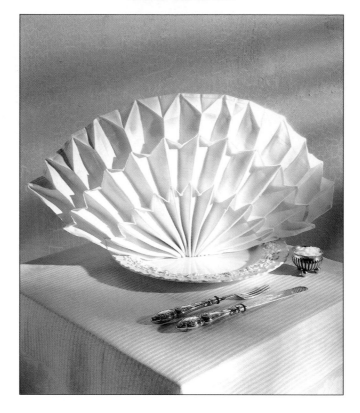

**B**

Ballerina 20
Beaded Napkin Ring 21
Bishop's Hat, the 47
Bow Tie 34
Breakfast Fold 32
Butterfly, the 63

**C**

Candle Fan 59
Candle Fold 53
Circular Napkin 36
Copy-cat Napkin Ring 10

**D**

Deco Fold 56
Decorated Napkins 22
Double Cornet 49
Double Jabot 44

**E**

Envelope 33
Everyday Fold 31

**F**

Fan, the 62
Festive Napkin Rings 14
Floral Napkin Ring 16
Four Feathers 52

**G**

Gingerbread Man Envelope 28
Golden Leaves 18
Guard of Honour, the 61

**J**

Jewelled Napkin Ring 25

**L**

Lacy Napkin Bow 13
Lacy Napkin Folder 11
Lady's Slipper 51
Lily 55
Lotus Blossom 42

**M**

Mitre 58

**N**

Net Napkin Ring 26

**O**

Oriental Fan 48
Oriental Fold 35

**P**

Palm Leaf 60
Peacock's Tail 40
Pineapple, the 39
Pocket Napkin 50
Pointed Pleats 54
Princess, the 46
Pure and Simple 43
Pure Elegance 45

**R**

Ribboned Napkin Ring 24
Ruffle, the 30

**S**

Sailing Boat, the 37
Stencilled Shell Napkin 17
Stiffened Bow 19

**T**

Tartan Napkin 23
Tassel Napkin Ring 15
Thanksgiving Napkin 12
Triangle Pouch, the 29

**U**

Umbrella, the 57

**W**

Waves, the 38